US

Handbook for Understanding Your Life

Dr. ANÍBAL P. SANTORO

Original title:

US

Handbook for Understanding Your Life

1st. edition, July 2023

Cover design and graphic art: Aníbal Pedro Santoro
Cover photography: "iStock.com/Irina Gutyryak"
Content review: Claudia Behn-Eschenburg
Style review: Romina M. Santoro Behn-Eschenburg
 and Alessandro V. Santoro Behn-Eschenburg

Made in the USA by

THINSCEN - The Inner Strengthening Center – Publishing House

ISBN 978-1-961728-11-0

US

Handbook for Understanding Your Life

Dr. ANÍBAL P. SANTORO

THINSCEN

Aníbal P. Santoro was born in Buenos Aires, Argentina, in 1960. He is a doctor in psychoanalysis, master in psychoanalytic psychotherapy, expert in metapsychology and psychoanalytic research from a perspective focused on individuals and their essential reality. He is also a certified executive and team coach and a lecturer.

He accumulates over 20 years of professional experience, being co-creator of the OntoPsyche® theory, axis of his onto-humanist school of psychoanalysis, based on which he has presented innovative works and given courses and lectures at international congresses.

He is co-author of the books *EnneaPsyche, One Among Nine*, the two volumes of *OntoPsyche - Beyond the Enneagram and the Psychoanalysis*, entitled *The Essence of Your Self* and *Your Dynamic Strengths*, and writes monthly in magazines in Latin America and South Florida, USA.

He is co-founder of THINSCEN, The Inner Strengthening Center in Miami, USA, accompanying people to transform their lives on a personal and professional level.

You can learn more about his career at
https://dr-anibalsantoro.com

Acknowledgments

To my wife, partner and colleague, Dr. Claudia Behn-Eschenburg, for being a partner in dreams with whom we build opportunities for the well-being of the whole family.

To my children Romina and Alessandro, Mariela, Natalia and Andrea, to my sons-in-law Mauricio, José and Andrés, and to my grandchildren Homero, Thiago, Luz de Paz and Río Maitén, for having allowed me to discover and confirm that playing a role is less important than being oneself for and with others.

To our students, for having understood our OntoPsyche® theory and for having wanted to participate and complete our exercises regarding the relationships that weaken or strengthen, experience from which I have obtained part of the material that today I include in this book.

To my patients and clients, who have allowed me to accompany them in some moments of their life processes, and have enriched me with their responses to each interpretation of what they were living.

Dedication

To all those who believe that an "*Us*" is more
than two people sharing a space.

Index

*If you relate to the result of
an educational or training process
and not to the people and
their essence,
you will be part of the problems
you will complain about later.*

INTRODUCTION

Us.

A single word given a fundamental value to society that can mean so many different things depending on how it is evaluated.

Although we are taught many things to condition our behavior so that we can live in society, the truth is that for many people the circumstances of their reality in a couple or in a group can burden them and hinder their transparent life process. Obviously, yours too.

This book was written for you, in the form of a manual, so that you have a counseling tool at hand for those moments when your "Us" may begin to weigh you down.

You will not find any advice here, because it comes from the experience of the person giving it to you. It is the familiar "What you need do is..." which, when you receive it, puts you on the side of those who know nothing, who understand nothing, who do not have the creativity to live their own lives, and so on. Of course, in the face of such moral support, you will probably feel inferior and worthless, and lose all hope because the obvious just has not occurred to you.

Perhaps there is one. I suggest that you open your mind to see situations from a different perspective.

I bring you "unconventional" points of view, critical and with different meanings that you will surely agree with.

The idea is that this will give you new tools to understand the value of the following sentence, so you can begin to immunize yourself against outside opinions and finally find your inner permission to be yourself.

The only thing we are all alike in
is the fact that we are all different.

In the following pages, we will address the social absolutes that intrude on your relationships, be they familial, scholastic, athletic, social, and/or professional. I refer here to the meaning you have internalized and established in relation to the "I", the "Other", and the "Us".

As you may have seen on the cover of this book, I have a doctorate, and it is in psychoanalysis. With what I have learned both in theory and in practice with my patients, along with the conclusions I have drawn that have led me to develop OntoPsyche Theory with my colleague, partner, wife, and friend, Dr. Claudia Behn-Eschenburg, I also bring you a summary of our theoretical approach so that you can understand your way of being, grounded, without moral debt, and most importantly, without guilt for being who you are.

I am aware that reading is not a common activity these days, nor is it everyone's cup of tea to read through voluminous volumes. For these reasons, I have tried to give you enough elements in this book to make you question and reflect on your behavior and attitudes, when you are in a relationship, so that you can judge whether you deserve to suffer the consequences of that behavior. In addition, you will be able to identify situations in which you are not faithful to yourself, put yourself off and accept treatments that you do not deserve.

To make the reading more agile and add even more value to the content, I have included QR codes.

All you have to do is scan each QR code with your phone to access an augmented reality that gives you clarity on concepts that might be difficult, not because they are difficult per se, but because they are the same, but viewed from a different perspective.

The most difficult part of any process to defusing limiting beliefs is identifying them and then facing the possible anguish of the void they leave when they disappear. It is always helpful to have data at hand to fill these gaps, because they help you to stop believing in what has been holding you back, and allow you to dare to change thanks to the support of your renewed certainties, strengthened by your own meanings.

Personal relationships become conflictual when one party submits to the other because one suffers while the other enjoys.

A key to avoiding or resolving these conflicts is to find out what reality means to each of us, regardless of what society and its culture have instilled in you during your educational process.

Because the education you have received is effective, it is very possible that you have moved away from your essence to learn that you are what you do or have, confusing your essence with the fleeting and ever-changing value of the role you play at various moments in your life.

For this review, I am also by your side, lending you my hand and accompanying you in the necessary process of taking a fresh look at all that you have learned about how life should be in a relationship and helping you to find your own meaning with which you can give new value to your life and your being you.

The benefit to you is that you can continue to be yourself, whether you are just with your "I" or integrating a "Us".

"I"

I Am a Unique Being

Why talk about the "I"?

The answer is simple. It is necessary because, despite the fact that "I" is the first person in terms of personal pronouns, we tend to shift before others who do not.

When we talk about interpersonal relationships in different areas, we do not realize that sometimes we beg for someone to see us and save us from our reality and need.

Your "I" is assaulted by the demands of your environment from the moment you are born.

As a baby, you want to eat without consciously knowing what it means to feed. However, there is no continuous nourishment and frustration takes shape.

You just feel that there is something that makes you uncomfortable and that you do not understand.

You have to act to get it out of you or to appease its attack.

So you cry, fidget, kick the air, and try to get attention in some way.

If you were born into an environment that did not seek you out, want you, and/or care about you, the response to your way of communicating for help will be slow.

You will have learned to activate your survival mode and respond to the environment according to the resources you bring in your genetic baggage.

If, on the other hand, you were born into a family environment where visions about the family, its *raison d'être,* and the meanings it has for its individual members coalesce into a fertile garden in which you can grow, the reaction will not be immediate, but you will learn that it always comes and reassures you.

Most likely you have almost no memory of this phase of your life, but much of what you read may have happened to you almost as I have described.

If you are in the situation of having to share your time with a baby, be sure to keep this in mind, because it will allow you to get in touch with what it cannot express other than the way it does. So you will be able to see that you are not contributing anything to the establishment of the life bond between the two of you if you evaluate and judge them as "tantrums" or "manipulations".

This is one of the "non-tips" I mentioned in the introduction, where I invite you to open your minds. Later, I will show you how it is that everyone has a certain view of life from birth to death that does not change and that serves as a guide.

As you grow older, two things will also grow with you, namely your self-confidence and your appreciation for yourself. By the way, you should know that these are the two pillars of self-esteem, which I like to define as the full awareness of all that you can do and/or accomplish.

As the years go by, the players around you change.

And this is where your access to your inner permission to think about what you have been taught not to question becomes increasingly important.

Your critical thinking and common sense are key to criticizing, suggesting, rejecting and accepting. All of these are among your most important tools and resources, those that sustain you as a strengthened individual with the ability to create new meanings and legitimize or delegitimize the authority of others before you.

Since we are talking about the "I", yes, your "I", stop and read the words used, because the ideas or concepts they contain are meant to give you more strength.

When power is exercised by the one who possesses it or claims to possess it, relationships with others are based on the effectiveness of subduing the will.

On the other hand, when power is transferred to a person through an act of legitimation, that person is invested with authority.

This is the power that every "I" has, including yours.

THE "OTHERS"

They are Unique Beings

To see these "Others" everything you have read in the chapter on the "I" remains valid. However, for reasons beyond this book, you can see more of yourself by analyzing the "Others" with whom you relate.

One of the many intervening elements by which human relationships are established and sustained is the ability to project our expectations onto the "Others"; this can be done in two main ways.

One of them is to become unaware of the "Others" and see them as a living canvas onto which to project one's anxieties, fears, demands, responsibilities, and even one's own frustrations, while expecting them to act in a helping, protecting, distracting, and/or saving manner.

The other modality is to use them as a mirror in which you see the reflection of what is yours and that you like or dislike.

In both modalities, these "Others" are succumbed. They disappeare, just as the screen disappears when you turn on the projector and watch the movie, or as the mirror disappears when it returns an image.

The "Others" are like You.

They have characteristics, motivations and beliefs, desires and ambitions, joys and sorrows, just like you, even if they are not the same.

The hard part is recognizing and accepting that the "Others" are not you and are just as unique as you are.

And the same thing You do, the "Others" do.

They also expect, project and reflect themselves onto you, and demand satisfaction of their needs and/or desires.

The "Others" make their presence known when this demand crosses the boundaries of what is natural to you and tolerable to some degree. When this happens, the "Others" become out of the enchantment that your mind created when you created an image of them within you and unconsciously decided that your relationship would be about them.

These "Others" are as real as you are.

Sometimes social distracters can dilute the weight that both your presence and the "other's" presence have on the other person, turning them into two familiar strangers who can equally evoke fascination or the deepest mutual rejection.

Those unique beings like You, who are the "Others," know of you only what they have invented for themselves.

Both know only the image they have made of each other in response to their own primary needs, which are tempered by the demands of life's circumstances at any given moment.

With such an image, both parties nourish their own hope of achieving what they each seek for themselves.

The "Other" is your partner, yes, as well as all parents and children, all teachers and friends, all bosses and co-workers.

In short, what you have read so far is something that is common to all people, without distinction of hierarchy; added to that, everyone is unique.

LOVE AND ITS 4 PILLARS

Trust

Respect

Abnegation

Demand

Four pillars on which love relationships should be based, including those of couples, fathers and mothers with their children, siblings with each other, children with their parents, the family in general, friends and other groups.

Four pillars on which love relationships should be based, including those of couples, fathers and mothers with their children, siblings with each other, children with their parents, the family in general, friends and other groups.

Later, I will show you that there are different natural and normal ways of being. However, it is useful to understand that every society, through culture and education, tries to smooth out these differences in order to limit possible incompatibilities and reduce the possibility of conflicts that prevent them from realizing their social plan.

Nevertheless, human beings come into the world with a baggage full of genetic resources that shape their capacity and ability to interact with the environment.

So, although it is a fact that our brain adapts to the demands of the environment, the genetic always remains and conditions the brain and hormonal structures, regardless of the induced changes.

For this reason, there are people who trust everyone by nature and without education. But there are also people who, by nature and without any reason that could explain it, distrust everyone except themselves.

Trust

When we talk about interpersonal relationships, trust refers to an inner state of certainty about what to expect from the other person.

This certainty, when it arises and is present, is usually described as a magic moment or a moment when the chemistry was right.

This is a delicate subject, because everything I wrote to you earlier is true, especially that concerning the formation of an image of the other person in you.

The initial trust arises for no reason; it is unconscious.

You cannot decide whether to trust or not, because trust means knowing something without having the data. However, the actions of the "Other" provide the elements with which to justify the consolidation or breakdown of trust.

This justification is a conscious act, nourished and strengthened by the perception of Respect.

Respect

As a value, Respect includes consideration and evaluation of the "Other," be it a person, an institution, or an idea.

In this understanding, there is no place for fear. Yet, many human relationships are based on the ability to incite fear and subjugation by pretending that the "Other" accept to be subjugated, having confused the meaning of Respect with the fear they feel of a perceived authority.

Respect is the sphere in which differences can be expressed without becoming a threat or conditioning factor to the relationship. That is, respect for the "Other" requires tolerance and acceptance.

When an external conditioning agent appears, such as a threat, blackmail, coercion, or even a reward, states of respect-fear and submission arise in the individual that are motivated by survival which weaken Trust.

Abnegation

This term usually evokes defensiveness because it is in some way associated with social and/or cultural demands that subjugate women. Please do your best to put this term out of your mind so you can continue reading the new perspective I am proposing.

Abnegation means denying oneself, giving up desires and interests in order to help other people.

Since the highest act of abnegation is to give one's life, it is associated with the idea of sacrifice and civic, military, and/or religious duty. For this reason, sacrifice is no longer considered a legitimate personal act, but a social value that is taught and required.

One problem with viewing it as a duty is that there are those who use it as an opportunity to control and subjugate.

Abnegation makes sense when both parties in the relationship benefit from it. Especially if you feel that you are better off having acted self-sacrificially than if you had not.

Demand

The thought of demanding something may seem extreme, for it implies that you are asking for something without the "Other" being able to refuse it; but it is not, for you are demanding what is due to you or what you think is due to you.

The idea of demanding can confront you with your current reality and history, with the culture and fears that have been instilled in you through upbringing. It points directly to your permission to demand what you want without having to explain or justify yourself.

It assumes that you are fully aware of who you are, what you need and/or want, and that you are clear about what you deserve.

Deserving is equivalent to being a creditor, having a right to something because you have fulfilled a requirement, whether social or existential.

Because you have gone through a process of education, the perception you have of yourself has been altered by the constant use of reinforcements to motivate or correct your behavior. In other words, you have been shaped by pure reward and punishment.

Remember that you deserve something only because you are a living being.

In pairs to balance

The 4 pillars of any relationship work well when they are balanced in pairs between the two of you.

Let me clarify the idea.

When I say "in pairs" I mean that both parties in the relationship must be able to show some level of commitment to each of the pillars.

When I say that the balance is "between the two," I am referring to mutually reinforcing pairs. So if the "Other" respects you, you respond by further strengthening your trust. When you are respected, you make the "Other" trust you more. This creates a back and forth that connects and strengthens bonds.

Trust ↔ Respect

There are other pairs that derive from these two fundamental pillars.

For example, if you have enough trust, you are not afraid to abnegate yourself naturally and voluntarily, because in this trust there is the certainty "without data" that the "Other" will not abuse you.

The Trust that people have favors their free Abnegation, without hesitation or fear.

Trust → Abnegation

On the other hand, Respect serves to contain the Demand so that it is not excessive and does not lead the "Other" into a position of submission or default.

So the Respect with which you treat "Others" means that your demands are contained and there is no danger of treating them wrongly.

Respect → Demand

Thus, the 4 pillars require a certain dynamic so that the relationships are balanced and fair for both parties.

The Respect of the "Other" towards me, nourishes my Trust.

The Respect of me towards the "Other" nourishes the Trust of the "Other".

Trust in me allows me to abnegate myself, whether sellf or in response to a demand from the "Other." Since this Demand is accompanied by Respect, it ends up strengthening the Trust in me.

The Respect of me nourishes the Trust of the "Other" and contains the Demand of me not to abuse the answer of the "Other" by Abnegation.

This ideal and possible circuit is, potentially, present in every human relationship. It should be clear that the quality of the bond and the vitality of this dynamic always depend on the strength of the natural personality of the parties involved.

Yes, while it may displease those who have the ability or need to control others, the most important thing that favors the possibility of constructive bonding for both parties in a relationship is the recognition and acceptance of the differences that make each person unique.

Neither a continuation nor an appendage of the other. Nor a shadow projected thanks to the light projected by the other.

In the same way, the people with whom you have to deal do not deserve to be considered less worthy than you, to stand in your shadow or dare to think after you have allowed them to do so.

The culture based on the rational management of fear, which seeks to promote the adoption of acceptable behaviors through the use of rewards and punishments, has led people to believe that they will only be accepted if they say and/or do what they have been taught they should do.

However, it is a mistake to rely on the outcome and effectiveness of a parenting or educational process while ignoring the essence of each individual. I have experienced this myself in my practice when I witnessed the serious consequences that my patients had to bear for this.

Considering that there is an Ontotype, the G-Skeptic, who distrusts everything and everyone, a strict education applied to the rest of the possible ontotypes leaves them defenseless against the attacks they might receive.

The reason for this is somewhat complex, but it can be summarized as people who naturally distrust others cannot contact or respect people. They merely create an image of them that they like and relate to them through that image.

As we have already seen, Trust and Respect are two pillars of love; therefore, the conclusion is that there are people who cannot love.

We have the opportunity to be and to make every relationship a unique experience by strengthening our own "I" and accepting the right of the "Other" to be strengthened as well.

I am a unique being.

You are a unique being.

And maybe we can make something wonderful out of that.

An Us.

Scan this QR code to learn more about this topic:

https://ontopsiquis.com/en/en-love.htm

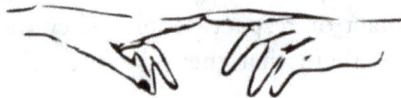

WHO'S WHO

We Are All Different

When the effect is the cause

The purpose of this section is to give you some additional elements to help you understand some facts that are often difficult to assimilate.

1) The essence of human beings does not change.
2) We are genetically determined to see life in a certain way.
3) Educating ourselves to live in a society can take us away from our essence.
4) We live in an effort to return to our center and overcome the deviation caused by culture.
5) "Perfect" people usually fight against the demons of their desires.

6) Being helpful is usually not free, and it is common to have to face a moral debt for the service received.
7) There are people who feel they "are somebody" only because of what they do and/or what they have.
8) Many give away their feelings, waiting only for an echo to confirm that they are alive to others.

9) Some need to understand and be able to explain the reality in which they live, precisely in order to live.

10) Those who do not believe in themselves when they are alone are very effective when they are in a group.

11) Those who believe in no one but themselves are very effective in manipulating those in the previous group.

12) There are those who take everything lightly and hope that the seriousness of life will never reach them.

13) Some conquer territories and organize their micro-societies simply because they know they can.

14) There are the conciliators, who make themselves available unconditionally to resolve conflicts or appease the advent of justice, even if it has nothing to do with justice.

As you can see, the diversity of natural ways of being, as well as the number of nuances that exist in this almost infinite spectrum, helps to shape what we call humanity; that is, "*Us*".

Below is a brief summary of the essential personality types we call *ontotypes*, described in the two volumes of our book *OntoPsyche - Beyond the Enneagram and the Psychoanalysis* entitled *The Essence of Your Self* and *Your Dynamic Strengths* from a perspective centered on the self and without judgments or diagnoses, along with a list of attitudes valued and to be worked on for each of them, contributed by our students.

Ontotype A – Educator

People with this ontotype tend to feel like masters of truth, with a natural permission to correct others and fulfill their mission to educate.

From an early age, they show an interest in knowing the rules that govern their social groups; they know the laws and interpret them to be able to apply them and respect them.

Similarly, with traditions; they enjoy the moment when they have to live them again, because that is the occasion in which they become the voice and the means to defend them, to respect them and to demand that they be known and respected.

They are both bearers and transmitters of traditions, rules and truth.

This last change of number to singular is important.

Truth.

As connoisseurs of the way things are to be done, they leave little or no room for the creative expression of an alternative solution in response to an event that requires action.

Many may see them as arrogant and inflexible, while others appreciate their ability to lead the way to completion by doing what needs to be done.

For them, doing the right thing is the only way to achieve the perfect, as they perceive perfection as the beacon that guides their thoughts, actions, and feelings.

Their high level of self-demand, constantly searching for both the error and effective ways to avoid or correct it, drives them to also motivate out of demand, resorting to phrases with teachings such as: "It's good, but it could be better," "Take responsibility and do it right, or better not at all," "Time is money," and/or the classic, "What you can get today, do not put off until tomorrow."

Their constant search for effective ways to achieve an ideal of their interests leads them to fight both against the limitations of reality and against those who accept them, without making any effort to get out of their conformist position.

They see life in terms of yes or no, black or white, without shades of gray or shades of other colors.

They organize, arrange, and plan events and resources so that the possibility of chaos or an unforeseen event is minimal or nonexistent. They anticipate and manage necessary resources according to their plans to avoid surprises that impede the achievement of a goal and/or affect their productivity.

They exercise an excessive amount of control over themselves that does not allow for spontaneity or play without rules; they are not guided by their impulses or emotions.

From their duty-based perspective, there is only the possibility of considering their access to gratification, or pleasure after they have fulfilled everything they had planned in their strict and extensive daily schedule.

Since the ideal of perfection has no place in the real world, they need a personal space where disorder is

41

possible; a permission for chaos and lack of control that can range from a simple desk or messy drawer to moments of alcohol consumption and/or sexual permissiveness. In other words, they control even the times when they can get out of control.

The following descriptive list of attitudes valued and to be worked on comes from a supervised and respectful vision of each natural way of being and acting.

Valued attitudes

- Straight Does the right thing
- Ethical
- Responsible
- Educator
- Controlled
- Disciplined
- Cares for money
- Organized
- Orderly
- Punctual
- Honorable
- Honest
- Someone to count on
- Prudent
- Predictable
- Dedicated
- Guidance
- Self-demanding
- Gives security

Attitudes to be worked on

- Perfectionist
- Irritable
- Demanding
- Impatient

- Believe they are always right
- Judge
- Educator
- Moralist
- Controlling
- Sexually repressed
- Rigid
- Strict
- Boring
- Superb (knows how things are done)
- Dissatisfied
- Normative

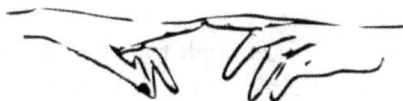

Ontotype B – Advisor

These people have the ability to build relationships based on devotion to others, with a helpful attitude and love. However, their level of devotion is of such a degree that it can cause some to enjoy their relationship as much as others feel oppressed and/or smothered.

The kind of love they offer and build the bond upon is always conditional.

In other words, they love in order to be loved, but with the special feature that they do not remain only with the possibility of receiving love. The dynamic that sustains their motivation to love is that they accept that if they are not loved, they at least expect to be loved. If they are not loved, it is enough for them to be desired, but if they are not desired either, they are content to be seen as necessary.

One could say that everything they do to serve the other, they present as a sacrifice that in some way requires a return in the form of love or gratification.

By giving love and getting it back, they feel acknowledged and accepted; something that they interpret to mean that they are chosen and that confirms to them that they are still a suitable alternative for a relationship. When this happens, a chain of mutual favors is set in motion. In this chain, everyone benefits in some way, since they tend to prevent the emergence of feelings of aggression or hatred by transforming them into more acceptable feelings associated with generosity.

Their generosity and altruism and services and attentions may be excessive, but they are not disinterested. They always demand recognition for what they have given.

If, instead of the expected treatment, they experience contempt or other kinds of mistreatment, they can show and return what they have received by making a series of demands in which they set forth everything they have done and all the sacrifices they have made in order to obtain the welfare of the ungrateful person who mistreats them.

You are adept at recognizing the wants and needs of others and thus seizing the opportunity to intervene and offer advice and guidance, even if it is unsolicited.

Their daily agenda includes a list of important events such as birthdays, anniversaries and other celebrations that they use to strengthen their social ties by being present with a detail, a phone call or a gift.

Just as a hand that caresses is in turn caressed, they offer themselves companionship when they accompany someone. For the same reason, they find it very difficult to recognize and accept boundaries. They easily resort to physical contact and flattery as natural means to build and strengthen bonds.

When people do not respond to so much caring and giving in a sustained, constant, or equal manner, they interpret this behavior as a threat that weakens the relationship and respond by sacrificing and giving more.

In this dynamic, they often transgress the obvious boundaries that define each individual's living space and may abuse each other's trust.

They are interested in being seen and regarded as very good friends; an accomplishment by which they evaluate the quality of their social life. They want their friends to talk about their qualities, recommend them, and allow them to expand their network to offer their advice and services. To this end, they strive to satisfy the needs of others.

Their spirit of sacrifice and devotion are the keys that allow them to get into situations where they can claim affective retribution.

They seem to take care of themselves when they take care of others, which is why they do not usually delve into their own emotional and/or self-related issues.

Valued attitudes

- Helpful Supportive Dedicated
- Charitable Generous
- Jovial
- Optimistic
- Expresses pleasant feelings
- Perceives the needs and desires of others
- Nurturing
- Sociable
- Cares for friends
- Effusive
- Kind Loving
- "Pretty-pretty", in a positive way
- Altruistic
- Detail oriented Observant
- Saving
- Attentive

Attitudes to be worked on

- Possessive
- Relationship opportunist
- Weed sower
- Postpones own needs and desires
- Avoids their own suffering
- Depends on what people will say
- Invasive, does not respect boundaries
- Non-committal
- Flattering Seductive
- Does not impose limits
- Gossipy
- Manipulative Blackmailer
- Gossipy
- Superficial False Unreliable
- Third party in discord
- Capricious
- Dramatic
- Overbearing (knows what needs to be done)
- Controlling Stifling
- Bill collector Spiteful
- Picks on other people's needs

Ontotype C – Model

They are enterprising, ambitious, demanding and highly competitive.

For them, winning is not a goal, but a certainty that guides them when they set out to do something. It's the only path to success they know: Understanding success on their terms.

When we speak of goals, they are not about winning for the sake of winning, but about being valued when they achieve it; their prize is not trophies, but the cheers and glory they gather.

Their personal commitment when they set out to achieve is total, because the value of the prize, as mentioned above, justifies any action that allows them to beat the other.

When they lead or compete, they can become role models, eliciting admiration, identification, indifference, criticism, or envy.

Since they are the most competitive of all ontotypes, it is understandable that giving up or withdrawing from a competition is not in their inner code.

In addition, they may become addicted to the activity in which they want to excel or have chosen in order to show off and be seen.

When they begin their race toward the goal they have set for themselves, they may neglect their personal lives.

Their emotions, desires and needs are a burden that can weaken them if they give them importance, because they divert their energy and distract them from achieving their goals.

They are ambitious people, for whom success is synonymous with acquiring goods that are coveted and valued by others, and receiving that value themselves.

In short, they do not feel that they have something of value by being themselves, but that they must do or have something in order to be of value.

Their satisfaction with an achievement always depends on the opinion of the public who sees them competing and winning; an opinion that, once received and internalized as a valuation, creates in them a feeling of not having enough value and fuels their need to want to achieve something more.

They idealize both those who succeed and themselves. In this way, they manage to compensate for their own devaluation and fuel their insatiable need to be special, admirable heroes who attract and capture the attention and admiration of others.

For the same reason, they tend to spend their time and effort on achieving goals that are not easy and require them to go beyond the limits of their physical endurance, receiving in return for so much effort another opportunity to avoid contact with their inner world.

Paradoxically, this emptiness that they feel and that they try almost desperately to fill requires an effort that seems unattainable for them. For in order to value and reward themselves, they would have to become their own audience and move away from the exterior, which demands more of them with every prize it gives them.

However, they navigate through life and society according to the image standards imposed by the sphere in which they wish to develop. They move away from their own essence, adapting like a chameleon to fashion and everything they discover that their potential audience values.

In fact, their path to success depends on the effectiveness of their ability to find out what people find attractive.

Valued attitudes

- Funny
- Flirty (dedicated to their image)
- Competitive against others
- Motivational Helps you stand out
- Fighter
- Role model
- Heroic
- Seductive
- Entrepreneur
- Salesman
- Positive
- Elegant Glamorous
- Attractive
- High self-esteem
- Persevering

Attitudes to be worked on

- Professional, with little affectivity
- False Hypocritical
- Arrogant
- Competitive
- Without limits
- Narcissistic

- Workaholic
- Committed and devoted to their image
- Chameleon-like
- Devaluator
- Depends on what people will say
- Seeks to be admired
- Loses self-respect
- Idealizes
- Appears grandiose
- Presumptuous
- Convenient Opportunistic
- Dependent on expectations

Ontotype D – Special

They are individuals who care about developing their identity, independent of external models of identification.

They know very well who they are and allow themselves to get in touch with their emotions, frustrations and feelings in a way that most people do not dare or cannot even imagine.

From this perspective and on an existential level, what is truly unbearable for them in expressing and sharing a part of their lives and feelings is the lack of the echo they expect from others. When faced with indifference and disregard from the environment, they quickly withdraw into themselves to seek refuge in their rich inner world that they have cultivated so well and in which they feel so comfortable.

Judgments can easily hurt them because they mean to them that they have not been accepted, that is, the denial of their being. Judgment for them is an evaluation of their obvious actions, but not of their meaning, motivations, or intentions.

They feel different and special because they have a high level of understanding of life and human relationships; a quality that distinguishes them from ordinary people because the latter do not usually deepen or signify life as they perceive it.

The valuation of their existence lies in what they can express from their emotions and feelings. Therefore, they usually do not attach too much importance to what they do or possess, because what matters is that others receive them.

Evidently, a familiar form of this kind of interaction with people, though not the only one possible, is artistic expression in all its manifestations, from acting to writing.

They are people attracted by the mysteries of existence, interested in discovering what lies beyond the visible and tangible, both in the esoteric, spiritual, parapsychological, mysterious or occult, as well as in the human psyche and in the interpretation of the unconscious world.

They are authentic beings, without masks, committed to the truth that lies in the essence of things, free from appearances and fashions, sensitive without reservations, passionate and esthetic.

Their intimate contact with their inner reality means that the social, i.e. the protocol by which people spend their time with others, having superficial conversations and/or little transcendence, is of no interest to them. This different way of relating to reality makes them feel like they are not understood, excluded from groups, or do not belong.

They retain the events of their life from the meaning they were able to elaborate on what they experienced, rather than from a simple description of them.

For the same reason, all their memories are recalled together with the emotions, feelings and affective reactions they have experienced. It is difficult for them to get away from it and even more so to forget the aggressions they may have experienced in their past.

On the other hand, this extreme sensitivity that makes them feel the depth and importance of life is the same sensitivity that they use to empathically connect with the people who approach them and give them the help they need.

They believe in love, generosity and kindness and refuse to accept that evil and cruelty are natural in human beings.

Naturally, they are intuitive and able to receive, process, transform and give back to each individual what they need to understand their reality and develop new tools with which to overcome and continue their lives.

Valued attitudes

- Sensitive Empathetic Intuitive
- Creative
- Artistic
- Honest Trustworthy
- Reliable Faithful
- Intense Passionate
- Continental
- Sensual
- Authentic
- Dreamer
- Detail oriented
- Kind Loving
- Humble
- Warm
- Devoted
- Introspective
- Respectful

Attitudes to be worked on

- Abusable
- Vulnerable Depressive
- Oversensitive (oversensitive)

- Feels guilty
- No defenses against pain
- Self-absorbed
- Retentive
- Frustrated
- Manipulable
- Feels misunderstood
- Emotionally helpless in front of others
- Asks for permission
- Feeling of not fitting in
- Justifies themselves
- Magical thinking (the other knows what I want)
- Demanding
- Fear of aggression
- Victim

Ontotype E – Explorer

People with this ontotype have their main strength in their mind.

They are mainly, thinking, cerebral beings, able to separate thought from feeling in such a way that the emotional part does not influence or interfere with their reasoning, in order to reach objective and well-founded conclusions.

The scientific method seems to have been written by and for them. They are able to deal with reality in a natural, analytical, and descriptive way because they have a superior ability to analyze and synthesize data and develop new questions, answers, and solutions.

They analyze reality by fragmenting what they perceive into small pieces that are easy for them to recognize and understand, in a way that allows them to determine both the potential threats and benefits and the resources they should deploy if they are confronted with them in their lives.

They store these fragments that result from their analytical process in their minds to create the image of a controllable space in which they can live without fear.

This "Departmentalization of Reality" that they perform in a natural, methodical and constant way is their strategy in the face of their tendency to be afraid of everything around them.

In this dreaded reality, there are also people and human relationships; complex elements of life that they process and transform into the data they need to connect on a purely rational level.

Before they are able to establish a relationship with another person, they must be able to "depersonalize" them; just as before they establish a relationship, they must "deaffectivize" the relationship.

Letting themselves be carried away by their emotions and impulses or spontaneously facing an unforeseen situation is an extremely difficult challenge, because it means giving up the protection of the mind and exposing themselves to the possible and unexpected in reality without the protection of thought.

These are capable people who work in research laboratories or in academia, who are usually misunderstood or the target of ridicule or diagnosis.

They are so engrossed in their logical processes that they are often seen as distracted from the demands of their environment, which is why they are diagnosed with attention deficit disorder.

This is a misconception, because they can concentrate, but only on what interests them and not on what is forced upon them.

This self-absorption and being locked into the realm of their reasoning and conclusions makes them forget their basic survival needs, which is why they depend on someone to take care of them and/or remind them that it is good to eat or clean themselves.

Social and cultural patterns, as well as habits in general, are of no interest to them, because their goal is social integration, that is, the reality they naturally fear and find difficult to accept.

Whether they are engaged in a scientific activity or something as simple as modeling, their way of interacting with reality is the same.

They are geniuses beyond IQ; they can see what other people cannot. This last characteristic explains their natural talent for teaching, because they do not recite or repeat theories, but teach how to think in order to draw new conclusions about the subject they are teaching.

Valued attitudes

- Intellectual
- Analytical Deductive
- Reclusive
- Eloquent
- Authentic
- Intellectually autonomous
- Knowledgeable Expert
- Objective
- Rational
- Knows how to focus and find what is important
- Meticulous
- Methodical
- Observant
- Scrupulous
- Ethical
- Intellectually ambitious
- Moral
- Specialist
- Scientifically minded
- Erudite

Attitudes to be worked on

- Insensitive

- Unattached
- Self-absorbed
- Neglected
- Abandoned
- Socially awkward
- Dependent
- Inconsiderate
- Jealous and greedy of his time
- Secretive
- Intellectual narcissist
- Devaluating
- Socially insecure Shy
- Depersonalizes (sees a person as a piece of data)
- Non-flowing
- Disaffective (sees a relationship as a piece of data)
- Selfish

Ontotype F – Loyal

They are loyal, responsible, sensitive, and grateful people who balance their fears with the security that belonging to a group gives them.

They have very little confidence in themselves. They subject the few certainties about reality that they can obtain to the analysis of their doubts and uncertainties, and so are caught in indecision and sometimes in inaction.

They feel safe when they are part of a group in which there is one or more people they can trust, because they need someone to take responsibility for the actions they are asked to take.

Their loyalty and voluntary submission to the authority they have chosen as leader make them very effective. Their behavior is similar to the well-known "due obedience" of military groups.

They are solidary and trustworthy when entrusted with tasks, provided they have been given clear guidelines for their execution and have the backing of an authority that cares about the consequences that may arise.

Behind their fear, which is exacerbated by their low self-confidence, they are warm and affectionate people who seek guidance and protection as long as they feel useful to others.

They usually do not argue about orders or question instructions, but doubt their own initiative. For this reason, they feel comfortable and safe while learning, fitting in, and performing routine tasks.

They think that by their obedience they exclude any possibility of error, as well as any liability if any should arise. After all, they have done what someone in authority has told them to do.

There is a tendency toward a conservative view of the facts of life, culture, and the direction of a society. Living within the known, doing the tried and true, allows them to relax and not be so cautious and pessimistic.

This defense of the known, which brings them security and peace, can lead them to extreme positions when they feel that their group membership may be threatened by an external action.

When this is the case, they consider that the group and belonging to it have more value than any truth to the contrary, even if it is scientifically proven.

They anticipate problems that do not always occur. They expend their energy dealing with their doubts and assumptions while building defensive structures to respond to what has not yet happened and most likely will not happen.

When faced with the imagined or real possibility of a catastrophic situation, from their perspective the only certainty is that the worst will happen; they feel exposed, fearful, and helpless in the face of inevitable calamity.

Even if they are able to save and are financially secure, they feel that they are impoverished and will not be able to create a secure and promising future for themselves.

For this reason, they tend to look for formulas that tell them what to do or how to proceed. They listen to and rely on the words of astrologers, psychologists, parapsychologists, graphologists, teachers, priests, relatives, friends, or others who might mean something to them or be an acceptable authority.

Something that may frighten them is the possibility of having to make their own decisions.

Valued attitudes

- Sensitive
- Loyal-Faithful
- Generous
- Responsible
- Meticulous
- Accepts that they are afraid
- Reliable and able to be trusted
- Delivers what is expected of them
- Grateful
- Supportive
- Cooperative
- Seeking links
- No malice
- Warm

Attitudes to be worked on

- Undecided
- Moldable Convenient
- Doubtful of everything
- Insecure Fear of own initiative
- Self-doubting (hypochondriac)
- Obsessive
- Fearful
- Pessimistic
- Stressed

- Dependent
- Complainer
- Naive Without malice
- Shy Pitiful
- Routine
- With a tendency to mediocrity

Ontotype G – Skeptic

They are naturally distrustful of everything and everyone, both events and intentions. They are meticulous, perfectionistic, and focus on details in order to dominate the reality that surrounds them and thus gain control over situations and people.

They are always ready to disarm any enemy. They create crises that destabilize others, especially when there are moments of calm to achieve their own stability.

The concept of stability is different from that of security. While the latter refers to the possession of one or more networks of guarantees, stability is strengthened by the detection, identification, control, and/or elimination of any source of threat or danger.

Because of their low or almost non-existent trust in other people, their personal view of themselves and life events takes on the value of an absolute truth. Seeing themselves as the "bearer of truth" somehow structures their psyche.

This distrust of anyone who is not themselves is fueled by a deep fear and a sense of having to live on constant alert, anticipating attacks and being able to defend themselves by striking first.

The counterpart to their distrust of others is their extreme self-confidence and natural ability to interpret rules and laws; of course, from a perspective that is convenient to them, allowing them to have and maintain control in their various groups.

They may feel as comfortable or even more comfortable in such groups than at home with their family.

They have minds worthy of a detective, and see in every situation the possibility of hidden intentions; hence their systematic and generalized form of doubt is their tool and their defense.

They take nothing for granted or for certain.

Because of these characteristics, they are highly sought after in organizations because they can anticipate problems and manipulate people, both to attract them and to control and restrain them. They tend to do what is necessary without letting their emotions or feelings distract them from what they are trying to accomplish or what they are being asked to do.

When their minds are not busy, they have time to dwell on their fears and are full of worry.

They are adept at developing and formalizing alliances. Even when they do not trust others, they find it very helpful to have one or more people close to them on whom they can offload their tensions and/or responsibilities.

They are unlikely to take responsibility for the consequences of a mistake they make because they can easily turn the situation around to present it in such a way that the responsibility and/or blame falls on someone else.

They are usually well accepted in social groups, as they always have the right joke or funny remark ready to defuse tensions in a meeting. However, their relationship with their own family can lead to conflict, as they want everything and everyone under their control.

Valued attitudes

- Responsible
- They are very social and charming
- Analytical
- Professional
- Strategist - Resourceful - Planner
- Achieves his goals
- Comedian - Humorist
- Detective - Daredevil
- Bold - Reckless - Adventurous
- Detects weaknesses and strengths

Attitudes to be worked on

- Seducer
- Abusive parasite
- False victim
- Cruel sadist
- Destructive
- Despot
- Complainer
- Controlling
- Strategist
- Victimizer
- Doubtful of everyone (paranoid) Distrustful
- Unable to love
- Explosive Discharges with violence
- Detects opportunities to attack
- Convincing
- Manipulative
- Counterphobic to decide and act
- Inferiority complex
- Hidden fearful Coward

- Loyal-Traitor Two-faced
- Hunter
- Obsessive
- Envious
- Resorts to manic defense: (control triumph omnipotent devaluation)
- Reacts negatively to expectations directed towards self

Ontotype H – Hyperactive

They are jovial, active, restless, and eager for all kinds of stimuli that entertain them and allow them to live without emotional or emotional gaps.

Their agile minds are constantly creating and connecting ideas in a tree with almost infinite branches; something that marks them as very good projectors, thinkers, dreamers and planners.

They have a hard time finishing the projects they start, because for them the fun is in the journey and never in the arrival. For this reason, they tend to abandon or postpone their project when it is close to completion because their mind is already absorbed in the details of the next project.

In their eyes, they are eternally searching for happiness. For them, happiness is the absence of sadness and any situation that requires an emotional response of pain, despair or anxiety.

This makes them good masters of ceremony. They are adept at detecting the level of prevailing mood at any gathering, party, or event and suggesting timely actions to lift the general mood.

Their thoughts are usually set in the future and can rarely be in the here and now.

The reason for this is very simple and has nothing to do with being distracted, but rather with having to respond in the present to an affective or empathic demand that exposes them to sensitive internal mobilization.

In other words, the present represents an almost certain threat to them of being confronted with emotional pain.

When they are in the realm of their mind and absorbed in their projects, they are free and happy.

They enjoy the expectation of everything that could happen. At a party, they are attracted by the mystery behind the possible fate of the celebration.

Since they live escaping from emptiness, excess is the only way left for them to get pleasure. Nothing reaches or satisfies them completely, because to feel satisfied they would have to be present and receive what they experience.

These excesses can be of any kind and exclude nothing, from meals to outings, from fashion news to jokes, from relationships to books.

Nothing seems to be enough, but everything works.

When they need to interact with another person, they often find the natural and normal pauses between sentences threatening and fear the affective response that might be required of them. Then they fall back on the treasure trove of resources they have. They may use a new joke or a quote from a book, a piece of news or a secret that a friend has confided in them.

There is no malicious intent behind breaking the secret and revealing something confidential, just their

69

desperation from the possible obligation of having to deal with a possible emotional pain they fear they cannot overcome.

They enjoy competing against others not so much for the prize, but for the adventure they imagine they will experience during the competition, as well as the opportunities for cheating or mischief.

Anything goes to have fun.

The premise is not to suffer, and through the entertainment they feel that they have achieved happiness.

Valued attitudes

- Fun
- Generous
- Social
- Entertainer
- Master of ceremonies
- Friendly
- Chatty
- Cheerful
- Friendly
- Optimistic
- Enigmatic
- Seeks to be happy by generating distractions
- Relaxed
- Mischievous

Attitudes to be worked on

- Avoid feelings
- Does not live in the now, lives in the future
- Too social
- Controlling

70

- Fears inner pain
- Superficial
- Hyperactive
- Plans everything
- Egocentric
- Ironic
- Wasteful
- Insatiable
- Easily bored
- Moody
- Demanding

Ontotype I – Territorial

They are competitive, providing and protecting people who know about the power that is in them. They are adventurous and passionate, able to commit excesses and get carried away by their impulses.

This natural awareness of their power and what they are capable of achieving often confronts them with situations that are almost impossible for other people, but which they know they can accomplish.

Many may judge them as overbearing or omnipotent. However, when a challenging situation arises, they usually achieve their goals, regardless of whether they have sufficient resources or had to create them.

So much power has a weak point, which is in the expression of love. They feel that love puts them in a position of vulnerability that weakens them.

To avoid this feeling, they rigidify themselves and cover themselves with impenetrable armor that protects them on the one hand and makes them unattainable on the other.

If they feel the need to ask for something, they feel deprived. If you want to give them something, be it a compliment, a caress, or anything else they have not asked for, it is not natural for them, nor is it easy for them to accept and receive it.

In short, they are good protectors and providers, but it is very difficult for them to receive something they have not asked for.

Because of the security that comes from being aware of their power, they often have difficulty accepting rules and laws that apply to everyone because they do not consider themselves part of the common.

They do not like feeling restricted or controlled, and they do not like being told what to do. When this happens, they can act out their anger without controlling themselves or thinking about the consequences of their actions.

They often form their micro-societies where their own law prevails, as if they were fiefdoms where feudal lords care for and protect the inhabitants of their citadels.

They are direct and effective, impulsive and tenacious warriors, grateful both to those who fight alongside them and to those who choose them as opponents to face in battle.

They are the only ones who can be considered authentically vengeful.

They accompany all those they consider their dreams, the brave and, in general, all those who dare to achieve what they want or need.

They do not tolerate cowardice, lukewarmness, mediocrity and certainly not betrayal.

Since they have nothing to prove to others or to themselves, they have a natural leadership whose accomplishments are free of self-interest. The targets they conquer, however, increase both their physical territory and the human base of their loyal following.

Once they begin a campaign, they do not stop until they have achieved what they want to achieve. They feel more motivated when challenges or difficulties arise, or when someone tells them that what they are striving for is not possible.

Valued attitudes

- Protective
- Strong Powerful
- Fighter Aggressive Hardy
- Resilient
- Passionate
- Self-confident
- Provider of means and tools
- Natural leader
- Spontaneous
- Empathetic
- Motivator
- Affective
- Tenacious
- Persevering
- They detect the needs of their own
- Defenders of their own
- Honest
- Reliable

Attitudes to be worked on

- Violent
- Impulsive
- Terminating (with me or against me)
- Visceral
- Authoritarian
- Vindictive
- Proud
- Inconsiderate
- Tough

74

- Cruel
- Radical Without measure or middle terms
- Tough
- They follow their own law

Ontotype J – Harmonizer

They are people who are ready to intervene in any situation to avoid conflict and injustice without expecting anything in return.

Strangely, they do not protect themselves from abuse or mistreatment, while they can expose themselves to defend others.

They have a natural ability to adapt to conditions that the average person would not endure for long. This hyper-adaptability is both their best competitive advantage and their greatest curse.

By adapting to anything without conditions or resistance, they make it easier for someone to abuse them. And as they compete with themselves, they themselves set up the trap they get caught in when they try to prove they can hold on a little longer.

Where others tire and give up, they hold their own. Because they have a special way of dealing with time, they are sure that the impossible will take just a little longer.

This way of dealing with time has positive and negative aspects of which they seem unaware.

On the one hand, it allows them to get out of conflictual situations, where stress and desperate reactions are the worst option, with virtually no signs of emotional wear and tear.

However, they are judged as procrastinators because their subjective conception of time may conflict with the time required to complete a task.

The problem of being judged is something that can affect them deeply as they strive for peace and harmony. They do not like to be seen as the cause of a problem or conflict, nor do they like having to explain themselves.

They give their all without holding anything back to protect themselves from any opinion that tries to blame them for what is a difficulty or harm to others.

They are autonomous, self-motivated, self-controlled and self-disciplined.

All of these "selfs" coupled with the fact that they very rarely communicate their needs, make it impossible for others to know what they need. They do not give any clues as to what needs become visible and serve as an access to their being.

They do not have great highs and lows. They are self-contained and uniform. They enjoy what they live without the outsider being able to easily recognize their joy.

Of course, for them there is always a way out of any pressing, stressful or difficult situation, so their attitude towards life is positive and realistic, not optimistic.

In the search for peace, they can withdraw and renounce any protagonist role in order not to become the cause of conflicts.

They have the ability to distance themselves from reality, avoiding contact with aggression and their own anger, and develop passive-aggressive behaviors that often lead to great conflicts, although they actually wanted the opposite.

Valued attitudes

- Likes to be who they are
- Loves unconditionally
- Calm Balanced
- Cordial
- Carrier of a natural positive outlook on life
- Tolerant
- Patient Time is their friend
- Altruistic Generous
- Conciliatory
- Empathetic
- Happy
- Flows with life
- Light-hearted
- Selfless
- Hyper-adaptable
- Uniformly passionate about life
- Can get sad, but not depressed

Attitudes to be worked on

- No room for self
- Is not loyal
- Fears, runs away from or denies conflicts
- Passive-aggressive
- Submissive
- Stops the world when it cries "enough".
- Self-denying
- Hyper-adaptable
- Detaches from the reality that demands it
- Responds to their own time
- Easily dispersed
- Absent-minded
- Seemingly dispassionate
- Negligent
- Seems tired or listless

Differences that unite and divide

So far, I have presented to you the general characteristics of the 10 main forms that the essential personality types or ontotypes can take. However, it remains to clarify what makes this bundle of abilities to define the possibility or impossibility of forming an "Us".

The answer lies in intrinsic motivations, as they are called in psychology.

In colloquial terms, it is what naturally moves people to action from their essence.

If the profile of people tends to fear, they will hesitate when they see a bridge that they have to cross, because their natural fear will erase any other possible representation and/or idea of usefulness on that bridge.

On the other hand, the same bridge will be seen as an opportunity to achieve their goals by people who have mastered their power and are used to competing and conquering.

And so we could continue to use this bridge and its possible meanings with each of the 10 ontotypes.

This mobilization from within, this unconscious motivation that occurs without warning or awareness, responds to the needs of every human being.

But they are not needs that arise from circumstances that occur every day. They have nothing to do with the demands of the environment or with the answers that must be given to life when an emergency, an urgency, or an interruption of the transparent flow appears in our path.

These are needs that are consistent with the natural way of being, that is to say, that which is at the base and never attained, displaced or extinguished by education or the cultural sieve.

We call them Primary Needs, making it clear that they are all different and that, as with ontotypes, none is better or worse than another, and none is right or wrong; apart from what is or is not convenient for the person who needs to give an opinion about them.

These differences seem beside the point, but they are not. After all, everyone has the right to see life as they "may" see it.

Intrinsic motivation based on primary needs is as misunderstood as it is powerful.

It is widely believed that people can be persuaded with money or some kind of momentary advantage to perform a task that they would not normally do without that incentive.

However, the unconscious quest to satisfy primary needs is powerful enough to break through the external conditions designed to get the person to perform behaviors, attitudes, and/or actions that others need.

People become demotivated very easily and quickly when any activity violates the satisfaction of the primary need. The logical consequence is that they begin to perform poorly, make mistakes, and even quit or leave their jobs.

At the relationship level, things get a little more complex when we realize that relationships also mean different things depending on the ontotype.

In our theory, we define three groups in which the meaning and importance of other people and the relationship with them are distinctly different.

The first group is people who are naturally empathic.

The emphasis here, as in all that I read to you, is on the word "naturally."

It's not about taking classes to learn how to pay attention to a person or how to respond to them so they feel considered. These methods may be useful for other purposes, but they are ineffective and insufficient at the level of interpersonal relationships.

Natural empaths are able to resonate with the other person, feel their emotions, suffer with them, and rejoice with them; most of the time even without a word.

This group of people includes the D-Special, I-Territorial, and J-Harmonizer ontotypes. They base their perspective on life and relationships on wanting, feeling, and acting on a sincere interpersonal level.

This group of people includes the D-Special, I-Territorial, and J-Harmonizer ontotypes. They base their perspective on life and relationships on wanting, feeling, and acting on a sincere interpersonal level.

A second group consists of people who defend themselves against others and relate only to the image they have created in their minds of others.

Fear is present in all of these ontypes in some form. They are able to recognize the fear of unconscious impulses or even fear itself, and rely solely on others, themselves, or the outside.

For these people, life becomes a daily struggle for survival that can only be achieved by developing their ability to structure, organize, stick to routines and agendas, and control.

They are natural administrators and researchers, for whom human relationships represent situations that must be understood, regulated, and used in some way for a useful and convenient purpose. They are people who think rather than feel their emotions, and they are driven by duty.

The A-Educator, E-Explorer, F-Loyal, and G-Skeptic ontotypes belong to this group.

There is a third and final group, that of people who invest in their relationships and image in the world, giving to others while expecting something in return for their investment.

They are very social and tend to pay attention to what others think.

Although they are very social, their emotional life is strangely overshadowed by the importance they attach to their social life and appearance.

In this last group we find people with the B-Advisor, C-Model and H-Hyperactive ontotypes.

Now we can better understand how these compatibilities or incompatibilities in relationships come about.

Each of the 10 ontotypes has its own primary need, and these are the following:

A	Educator	- To be perfect
B	Advisor	- To be loved, wanted, or needed
C	Model	- To be valued
D	Especial	- To be
E	Explorer	- To be an expert
F	Loyal	- To be secure
G	Skeptic	- To have stability
H	Hyperactive	- To have happiness
I	Territorial	- To have power
J	Harmonizer	- To have peace and harmony

Remember that each of these primary needs is independent of the circumstances that each individual has to live.

To understand it better, think about what you need when you do not need anything; that is, what motivates you to do something when everything is fine.

Although it may seem utopian to think that everything could ever be fine, the fact is that even when you have a need that must be satisfied, such as earning money to pay your debts or getting a job, even in the midst of all these environmental demands, your primary need will continue to dictate the course of your decisions and fight from within against the superficial motivations that deny, threaten, or contradict it.

This means that the formation of an "Us" is not so simple or simply depends on being carried away by a
84

force of attraction or obeying an external command that requires us to work as a team.

In team coaching, it is important to recognize these profiles that are characteristic of each essential personality type.

A team is a cohesive group. The most important element to achieve this cohesion is the establishment of trust between the members.

However, we have already seen that, for example, Skeptic trust anyone, and we have also seen that their characteristics make them one of the most sought-after ontotypes in companies.

They are the most skillful survivors, able to use anyone to make profit without feeling any kind of guilt or remorse for this attitude towards the other.

It is very likely that people with this ontotype can be found in any group, so transforming a group into a team can be a long, arduous and unsuccessful task if not detected in time.

Moreover, it must be kept in mind that their greatest success is to remain undetected in their true nature, because the less others know about them, the more defenseless they are.

Their primary need for stability seems to give them the natural right, as survivors, to do and take whatever they consider to survive.

At this point it is important to emphasize that each ontotype has its own primary need and that each ontotype is based on a set of strengths.

The point is to recognize them, accept them without judgment, and strengthen them.

"US"

We Are the Other With Me

And I With That Other

It seems easy to start a relationship because it would be enough to let go, flow and then see what happens.

This "then" is the key that can help you avoid heartbreak in your relationship.

Let me clarify that the comments I give in this chapter are only a description of possible situations and do not correspond to a personal position nor imply any kind of judgment.

When I lived in Mexico, I often heard the slogan "Échale ganas" in my practice, which in English means "Do your best."

Believe me, it is a misconception promoted by the culture through the necessity of a society that cannot stop at every family conflict.

If you have to "put your heart into it," the relationship most likely ceased to exist some time ago. Another folk wisdom confirms what I say: "By force, not even the shoes fit".

In a relationship there are two beings, two wills, two different ways of thinking and dreaming, each going their own way.

Sometimes they attract each other and sometimes they repel each other, but the course of their encounter continues to respect and honor the signpost that gives them a common goal that stands above their individual desires, as long as both continue to move forward.

Unfortunately, this common goal that unites the couple is very difficult to define because it is intangible. It is the result of a tacit agreement in which the words were not spoken because the essence of the members had already understood everything.

It often happens that the beings who are going to meet or who have already decided to leave their traces together have become distant from their essence and are connected only by their roles; they have lost any possibility of understanding the meaning of their union.

The encounter between people on the basis of the roles imposed on them by culture inevitably leads to the dissatisfaction of one or both parties. Sooner or later, one or both will try to stop and analyze what they are doing or achieving by being part of this couple, and they will weigh the benefits of ending the relationship.

In the case of these couples, the common goal on which they based their relationship was not intangible but quantifiable; that is, they could have agreed on an allowance, a big house, lots of cars, or a big bank account. All visible elements used to evaluate the success of the family cell, onto which society could project its own success.

Until a few decades ago, women were given lessons to learn how to be good wives, housewives, cooks, and even mothers.

That has changed.

Men are still educated from the perspective of the one who must provide for them.

The latter is still the case, but is confronted with a global economic reality that requires men to accept being unemployed or underemployed, while women go to work in positions once reserved for men.

Behind the mask and the expected function of a learned role there is only emptiness, the same emptiness perceived when partners find that they cannot have a conversation in which they receive the other fully, without defenses or reservations, or that they cannot exchange more than complaints about what they have experienced during the day or at work.

Much less connection, or the possibility of it, is observed when there is a sense that someone needs to take rescue action to save or help the interlocutor after listening.

Perhaps this void of empathetic words and silence is masked or filled with sexual activity, parties, alcohol, outings, children, or other distractions.

If the couple has had to accept the entrance of a distractor, perhaps something is wrong in the couple. The connection, if there ever was one, that allowed them to build options for their life together may have been lost.

To be in a couple and being a couple are not equivalent concepts.

If you are in a couple, it could be said that you have provided for the satisfaction of some aspect of your life and that you may also have agreed to provide one or more benefits to the other person you are with.

The idea in the paragraph above comes from an actual event I participated in, and it was the first time I heard something that was so incredible to me that it took me a long time to grasp it.

A few years ago, I was interviewed on a radio program in Mexico City, which gave me the opportunity to present and talk about our first book, *EnneaPsyche, One Among Nine.*

During the presentation of our perspective, which focuses on the innate characteristics of human beings rather than the result of the education they have received, one of the panelists confronted me with my approach by arguing that marriage was, after all, nothing more than an economic arrangement that guaranteed certain desirable conditions.

From his point of view, the desire of two beings to share their lives in communion, whether married or cohabiting, was nothing more than an opportunistic contract in which feelings were an obstacle.

I remember being speechless.

He went on to explain both the sexual benefits of a couple not having to go out of their way to find someone with whom to satisfy their needs, and the benefits of an arrangement in which the woman can make of her life what she wants, as long as she adheres to cultural, marital, and social guidelines.

It is clear that today, almost twenty years later, if he had made these remarks publicly, he would have been censured and even sued.

When I recovered after hearing what was inadmissible for me, I could answer him that our theory explains exactly that there are people who can see life and relationships from his perspective, and that there are also people with a different point of view and a different way of making contact on a human level.

For some reason, he remained silent for the rest of the program.

This anecdote I share with you is to show you that although we have all received some kind of education with many or few similar aspects, in human relationships it always depends on who each individual is.

As in this example, it is very likely that this panelist "used to "be" in a couple; but we know nothing about the other member.

If it were the case that the one who accompanied him also had a similar approach, both would take advantage of the situation and "hoard" the benefits they hoped to gain.

Practically, they function like an economic-productive cell in which the partners make some profit in exchange for generating wealth and competing for survival.

It is clear that later, in a divorce, this cell will be confronted with the division of what it has earned in order to continue; as if its members had only lived through an economic cycle in which they bet on a dream that has borne some fruit, which they may say has failed and that it is over.

They are in a couple and they last.

They endure and bear as long as necessary, as long as the goals are achieved or the life cycle of the agreement between the parties is fulfilled and the partner company decides to request its dissolution.

92

We are in a time of profound change where everything is being questioned.

There is a political agenda that supports social reengineering and seeks further change to ensure the achievement of goals whose understanding is beyond the capacity of the people who live day by day.

Political agenda or not, people remain as they were born and as each one of them is.

One can try to impose the fashion of "polyamory," but couples who are faithful and loyal to each other will continue to exist and form.

By calling this possible type of relationship a fashion, I am not passing judgment and am only giving a reading and description of what is happening in current history.

In Moses' time, when the world was depopulated, the prevailing slogan was "Unite and multiply."

Today, in a world of more than eight billion people, this slogan is obviously perceived as a threat that forces a rethinking of society.

In the midst of these global needs that seek to limit and manipulate what kind of couple to have and what kind of family to foster and/or strengthen, there are immutable elements.

You.

The Other.

And the resulting "Us" who must fight for their chance to be when conditioned or attacked by society and culture.

When the 334 allele is present in men, it is likely that they are more prone to polyamory or infidelity than men who do not have this gene.

Given this genetic reality, there is no political agenda or fad for transforming society to change the way these men relate to each other.

The man who avoids commitment, if he marries, will be looking for some kind of "relief," and if he does not marry, he is likely to have continuous, successive monogamy. That is, short and frequent relationships.

These are all examples of real possibilities that exist to give life to an "Us" according to the feelings of its members, without judging whether they are in a couple or if they are a couple.

At this point, then, it is time to talk about this other way of constituting an "Us", because there are also people who need and want to "be" a couple; who are able to be together while they are, and at the same time create a home. One for the other and with the other.

I often meet couples where one wants to be in a couple and the other wants to be a couple.

Somehow, in these cases, one of the parties remains subservient to the wants and needs of the other, not so much because of a bad disposition of one against the other, but because the expectations are opposite. While one wants to build a life, the other just wants to get through another day, with no expectations, only lasting and keeping a tacit imaginary agreement that has been created to receive guarantees and benefits.

It is common to talk about compatibility and incompatibility of characters, resorting to popular phrases that reinforce the need for further "effort," such as "love hurts," "opposite poles attract," "in every couple there is strife," or the well-known "there is nothing better after a fight than a good reconciliation there is nothing better than a good reconciliation," with its dubious implications in terms of obtaining an alleged sexual pleasure after an argument that could have been avoided.

As if by deciding to become a couple, one must resign oneself to standing in the shadow of the other's supposed brilliance and going where the other wants to go.

At this point, it might be useful to re-read the summary of characteristics I presented in the Who's Who chapter.

It may seem strange to you that these differences are real and natural, but I have seen and confirmed them in my own practice and in my supervisions with my wife, Dr. Claudia Behn-Eschenburg, about her patients.

Remember that no one changes for another, even if it hurts what you think or feel you are worth.

Also, think about what I showed you earlier in terms of groups of people with ontotypes who contact each other, or who relate to each other's image because of the different types of fear they feel, or those who invest in relationships.

People are born with an essential personality type that will accompany them throughout their lives. The rest are social layers, protocols product of education, lies that must be paid as a tribute to belong to society, that disguise, hide or try to dilute the strength of the natural essence inherent in each person.

Not everyone has the same energy, the same desire, the same sexual need for the other, the same expectations of the relationship and the same parameters for contact, evaluation and interaction with reality. All of this is what it is intended to be normalized, or rather standardized, by culture and the media.

Being a couple means seeing the other and seeing ourselves, seeing the other as they see us, and seeing ourselves as we see them.

I am not talking about possessing something, but seeing it; contemplating, admiring and receiving the immensity that encloses the other life that chooses to go through its own in our company.

In the "I see you" that the movie Avatar gave us, we find the same power or more than that which could comprise an "I love you"".

Those who are a couple, unlike those who are just there, usually have the flexibility to put aside their personal interests. I am referring to both parties abnegating themselves in favor of the common goal they have set for themselves; something that allows tolerance and understanding to emerge between the two of them.

Unlike the previous modality, when the 4 pillars of love are present and the couple lives in mutual tolerance and understanding, there is no feeling of wear and tear and the couple is built by renewing the decision to belong.

Obviously, with this kind of couple, the freedom to belong is the key.

Let me clarify this point.

Freedom can manifest in many ways because they all respond to some kind of decision. But we have seen that there are different natural and normal ways of being, regardless of the education one has received, adopting different points of view to understand and comprehend the same event.

When I suggested to you the example of the different meanings that can be assigned to a bridge, I also opened the possibility of completing the idea of what it means to choose an alternative.

Remember that in every decision you make, your primary need is always present, so that if you respect it in your decision, you will feel more vital to bear the consequences of your decision. This is what in psychoanalysis is an "egosyntonic" event, that is, what you do is in harmony with your "I," with who you are beyond your roles.

It is true that sometimes we have to decide in a way where we are neither satisfied with what we have decided nor with what we will face afterwards. We decide almost forced by circumstances and we do not experience a sense of relaxation or ease after we have decided. In psychoanalysis, this would be called an "egodystonic" event, meaning that what is done is not in harmony with the "I."

97

Choosing in freedom must be egosyntonic.

When you are a partner, you choose several actions and the acceptance of their consequences.

One of them, the most direct, is to choose the other.

Another is to choose to accept that the other has the right to choose us.

And another, perhaps the one that represents the leap of faith that most builds and strengthens the couple, is the decision to accept what the other has chosen.

Without conditioning or ultimatums; simply being open to make, give and receive, day by day, from one towards the other, from the other towards oneself, from one for the other and from the other for oneself.

The only way to live the couple in this way is from the free personal engagement of the two in it.

Note that, when talking about commitment, in a daily dynamic of rediscovering the other and of the free choice I spoke of before towards that person, there is no place to talk about gender.

Love based on commitment, fidelity, trust, respect, abnegation and demand is a love in which people are called to be a couple and to build life as each of them can and wants to.

The other possibility is an equivalent situation where people are in a couple without any commitment except to themselves and without respect, trust or abnegation. The only thing that matters is to feed the illusion of companionship while fulfilling the goals for which the parties have decided to become a couple. The important detail to consider is that they are only there, lasting, without wanting or being able to become a couple.

Since, as we have seen, there are ten ontotypes with different motivations and many genetic variants that manifest themselves in people's behaviors, it is necessary that you get in touch with yourself and not be afraid to make a mistake.

The worst decision is the one you do not make.

It is possible that after you dare to take the step to a new "Us", you do not like what you have lived or are living.

If that is the case, the first premise is to be faithful and loyal to yourself in order to save the rest of your life from the possibility of finding yourself lasting in a relationship marked by suffering.

Do not allow yourself to "put your heart into" the relationship because it probably no longer exists or may never have existed.

The characteristics of the ten ontotypes are immutable. Yes, it is true that there are certain manifestations and attitudes that can be "polished," but the engine that drives people's thoughts and feelings is the same throughout their lives, and no one changes their way of being in favor of another person.

All this is only part of the infinite number of traps that culture sets for us when it wants to teach us how to live.

In your being there is a code inaccessible to others that has the function of taking care of you, among many others.

The only way to prevent this is to change your perception of things. This happens when you are asked not to cry, not to scream, not to run away, not to be afraid, not... to be you.

You cannot possibly be you in a couple if you are not you with you first.

Return to yourself.

Learn what you can accomplish when you are alone, because in your physical solitude you will discover how important you are to yourself.

When you know yourself, get to know yourself again, and reach a point where you realize that you cannot live without yourself, you are already able to be with another person without the risk of being dependent, subjugated, isolated, devalued, and/or doubting that you can sustain your own life.

When you know who you are, there is no risk of being confused when people try to confuse you, because you know what motivates you because you know what your primary need is; that will always determine the way you perceive reality and the way you find interest in what life has to offer.

You are not immune to manipulation and never will be, but if you are sure of yourself, you will be able to recognize more quickly the signs that tell you that you should withdraw from a relationship that is not worthy of you and in which you will certainly put your dignity at risk.

If you enter into a relationship out of necessity, you will always be dependent on the other person.

On the other hand, if you know yourself and want to become a partner by being yourself, by doing this because you want to and not because you have to, you secure your independence; being able to be a partner as long as you keep the freedom to choose it every day.

These are the signs that threaten your sense of dignity. Every time you receive treatment that you do not deserve and you become aware of this fact, this treatment was not worthy of you. On the other hand, every time you deserved something and had to ask or beg for it, that treatment was unworthy of you.

As you can see, a crucial key to being part of an "Us" is in the awareness of your being, of what you deserve and what you do not deserve, how strong your idea of dignity is, and how clear you are about whether you are seeking the relationship because you are running from something or someone or as a means to achieve some other goal different from what it is to feel like you are in company while accompanying the other on a path of life building in which the difficult that might happen is tolerated but not suffered.

The possibility of living through a back-and-forth, where a pendulum movement is created that keeps the engine of shared life running without either of them disappearing, because both are the protagonists in this kind of dynamic to build an "Us", seems to have more possibilities to emerge in unions where members are motivated to be a couple.

But even if people choose to be a couple, or mutually commit to being a couple, there is always the possibility of cohabitation under certain conditions, if agreements can be made.

In an agreement, two wills join hearts and decide to perform a series of actions for mutual benefit.

Let us read this again.

Two wills...

In other words, the ability to reach agreement requires that there be at least two people in a given instance, reviewing the data at hand and evaluating the best strategies to achieve the greatest benefit.

Agreement is based on the ability to discuss and exchange points of view in a way that enriches both parties after they have absorbed each other's approach in order to conclude the discussion with a mutually agreeable decision.

When there is consensus, neither of those who have agreed on a strategy has the right to come across as the superior being who made the best choice, or to point fingers or blame the other for making a mistake in their decision and thus both have lost an opportunity to benefit.

Agreements are strengthened by consensus, and reaching consensus on a decision requires mutual respect.

Agreements can only be reached if communication is cultivated and practiced.

We are the agreement that lights the way and dissolves the shadows of disagreement.

We are.

Thank you for being the one who reads and receives me.

Thank you for being there and allowing me to accompany you to rethink what seems so simple and obvious, to see it from another perspective and give it another dimension.

You and I have made a connection between author and reader that has led to the creation of a new...

_Us_

P.S.:

I invite you to learn more about the 10 essential personality types and their 56 combinations with the following books:

OntoPsyche – Beyond the Enneagram and the Psychoanalysis
Vol I – The Essence of Your Self
Vol II – Your Dynamic Strengths

by Dr. Aníbal P. Santoro & Dr. Claudia Behn-Eschenburg

For further information and access to our books, please visit

https://ontopsiquis.com/en/en-index.htm

You may also be interested in reading about the benefits of using OntoPsyche to understand family dynamics:

FAMILY - The 7 Secrets to Your Best Family Life

by Dr. Claudia Behn-Eschenburg

www.ingramcontent.com/pod-product-compliance
Lightning Source LLC
Chambersburg PA
CBHW052053270326
41931CB00012B/2742